COME UNDER THE WINGS

COME UNDER
THE WINGS

A MIDRASH ON RUTH

GRACE GOLDIN

THE JEWISH PUBLICATION SOCIETY OF AMERICA
PHILADELPHIA
5718-1958

For Yudi
returned with thanks

I first thought I'd like the Midrash—a commentary on the Bible by rabbis of Greek and Roman times—when I read there that the heavens fit the earth like the lid on a kettle. Then I discovered Rabbi Eliezer, of the second century, putting the following words into God's mouth, in a commentary on the *Book of Ruth:*

> Boaz played his part, and Ruth played hers, and Naomi played hers, whereupon the Holy One blessed be He said, I too must play mine.

After this, I read the rabbinic *Midrash on Ruth* from end to end. It tells a story nearly as full of vitality as the biblical tale, though new and strange in many details to readers of the Bible; for to emphasize the miraculous role God played, the rabbis say Boaz was an old, old man when he begot his son Obed, and died in the very act; they speak of Ruth and Orpah as princesses in Moab, and of Goliath as Orpah's great-grandson, as David was the great-grandson of Ruth. Ruth herself, they believed, could not possibly have died without experiencing in full her reward for converting to Judaism—she must see with her own eyes David on the throne of Israel.

I wrote this poem to round out the rabbis' version of the story and to illustrate their point of view—

not with any thought of superseding the perfect, and perfectly well known, biblical *Book of Ruth*. My chief sources were the *Midrash Rabbah on Ruth*, and Louis Ginzberg's *Legends of the Jews*, though from elsewhere in Jewish legend I borrowed any fragments I needed that seemed to show the right rabbinic fire. Those familiar with the material will know, in the words of Yeats, "what debts I owe and to what creditor."

G. G.

CONTENTS

ON THE GOLDIN "MIDRASH RUTH"

The charming poem which Grace Goldin here presents to the public is an ingenious exercise in one of the oldest and most persistent creative literary forms known to the Jewish people, a form of which it is the peculiar and paradoxical merit that in order to appreciate its freshness one must first get the feeling of its antiquity. For those who are acquainted with the Midrashic contrivance these lines of explanation are unnecessary; others may find it helpful to a greater enjoyment of the book if they pause for an introductory moment to consider how it has come about that a tradition makes news.

The collection of writings which we call the Tanach, accumulated perhaps in the course of a thousand years and fixed in its final form some two thousand years ago, has retained until our day and seems likely to retain into the far future an astonishing continuity of contemporaneousness. To say that it is "a living document," and is that because it deals with eternal human prototypes and eternal human preoccupations, is to avoid the unique problem of this phenomenon. "Living document" is a figure of speech; it is applied to any record, and there are several such, in which mankind will always remain interested. Taken literally the phrase means a document which is actually alive, that is to say, has the biologic characteristics of a living thing: it grows, it develops, becomes something new to each generation while always remaining itself; it is, in other words, a perfect achievement in spiritual ecology. In this sense

13

the Tanach is the only "living document" of which we know.

The beginnings of the Midrashic tradition antedate the canon; they are already intertwined with the biblical text itself. When the Tannaim spoke of the "oral law" as coeval with the Torah, twin-delivered to Moses at Sinai, they were in effect asserting that the Tanach was born with infinite adaptability; and what was true for them regarding the Halakic or regulatory aspect was also true regarding the Haggadic or humanistic and folkloristic. In this assertion they created, or at any rate reflected, the durability of Judaism. The Sadducees disappeared because they were incapable of grasping and applying the life-giving principle of the "oral law," hence of the Midrash.

When I speak of the "contemporaneousness" of the Tanach I must not be taken to mean that its pronouncements, narratives, and characters can be tortured into current values. The fact that this has often been done merely testifies to the durability—as obvious as that of Judaism itself—of the ungifted scholar and the poet *manqué*. I mean, instead, that every generation, living in its own intellectual setting, struggling with its own problems, speaking its own ideological dialect, can find a natural mirror of itself in the Tanach. Mrs. Goldin observes in her preface that she had no thought of superseding the "perfect and perfectly well-known" Book of Ruth. Thomas Mann makes the same unnecessary disclaimer in regard to his *Joseph and his Brothers*. It was of course

14

the attitude of the Men of the Midrash. We are not dealing here with replacement or even restatement, but with rediscovery, the very point of which is that what we have "rediscovered" seems always to have been there; and the naturalness with which this point is made is the measure of the rediscoverer's skill.

It happens to be a rare kind of skill. Love of the Bible is not enough. Nor is it enough suddenly to get "a wonderful idea" for a Bible story, a "gimmick" on the accepted record; for not all Bible stories can be considered Midrashim. There have been, alas, many lovers of the Bible who ought to have kept their passion to themselves. What is needed, besides love and knowledge and inventiveness, is the instinctive capacity to blend the modern and the antique without offending either, to avoid equally the archly archaic for oneself and the jarringly anachronistic for the story. But above all the re-narrator must move in the spirit of the text; a wild and irresponsible inventiveness, a frenzy for "originality," are self-defeating; they end up rapidly as tediousness. It is a question of style in the widest sense, issuing from the correct relationship.

It is also, in homely phrase, a question of getting off on the right foot. Mrs. Goldin begins:

In the days the Judges judged in Israel
(God judge our purposes as He judged theirs!)
Two men of substance lived in Bethlehem,
Upright and canny, Bible millionaires.

15

It is the right touch; the reader breathes a sigh of relief and settles back. If he has long been pondering —and what Bible lover has not?—the thousand questions this particular scroll raises, he hopes to receive a certain illumination. To expect "answers" is too much; the riddles of the Bible were not propounded in order to be solved but in order to provoke everlasting scrutiny and self-scrutiny. It is enough to give ear to a fellow-seeker—the search is the thing. And in this instance the seeker has brought together from the chief sources the surmises of the seekers of the past. Here is a Midrash on the Midrashim.

And so the questions are in a way provisional, and it is the discussion that matters. What kind of man was Elimelech, the husband of Naomi, the father of Mahlon and Chilion? The text is silent, the Midrash reticent. Some of the hints Mrs. Goldin accepts, and with surmises of her own puts together a wholly coherent and tragic personality, a man whose high beliefs were frustrated by a low caution, who reaps in the apostasy of his sons the harvest of the mean shrewdness he displayed when he abandoned his native town and land to its troubles, and who must in despair end his own mismanaged life. Was this indeed Elimelech? For the given purpose, yes. He fits in. He is real. He is of our day as of his, and that is enough.

What manner of women were Naomi and her widowed daughters-in-law, Ruth and Orpah? To me Naomi is one of the most fascinating of biblical fig-

ures. What is perhaps the most beautiful speech in
the Bible is uttered by Ruth; but it is Naomi who
inspires it. Perhaps the most beautiful incident in the
Bible is the coming of Ruth to Bethlehem-Judah to
fulfill her rôle as the ancestress of King David and the
Messiah; but it is Naomi who arranges it. Leaving
out Providence for the moment, which is the instru-
ment here, whose the melody? The most courageous
depiction in the present poem is that of Naomi. Per-
haps for fear that her extraordinary gift for awakening
love might make of Naomi something unearthly and
unreal, Grace Goldin endows her with a touch of
sternness of purpose which, incidentally, brings into
painful contrast the weakness and confusions of
Elimelech. He, to save his sons' lives—or so he would
have it—chose the easy way for them, to their and his
undoing. Naomi, the Bible tells us, discouraged her
daughters from accompanying her back to the land of
her birth. Mrs. Goldin, following the Midrashim,
gives a larger compass to the discouragement. After
dwelling on her own played-out life (actually, as we
know, it was a life that was to burgeon into the
triumph of the late years—an everlasting reminder
that it is never as late as one thinks) she explains to
her daughters-in-law all that is meant, by way of suf-
fering and responsibility, in becoming Jewish; and
Orpah, as we know, turns back. Ruth, the undis-
courageable, is disturbed by her mother-in-law's un-
compromising explicitness. We read:

17

"You were too harsh with Orpah," Ruth declared.
"Had you but coaxed her as she dared you to
She might have gone the difficult way with you."

And Naomi makes the striking answer, reminiscent of the stern intellectual probity of a Job:

"We are forbidden bribery, my Ruth."

Ruth's conversion is celebrated in a powerful version of the Adon Olam. Mrs. Goldin does not attribute it to Naomi. I think she should have done so. Job-like too—but in how different a context—is Naomi's career, the complete loss and the complete restoration.

Mrs. Goldin's Ruth is invested with a spiritedness I had not thought of attributing to her. After a month in Bethlehem, where Naomi's calamities are regarded (we think of Job's comforters) as God's punishment for the misdeeds of Elimelech, Ruth exclaims:

"I am tired of hearing of the wrath of God,
I weary of divine recompensation."

One asks again, were these the actual personalities? And again we reply with the wholly satisfactory evasion: "Yes, they were these, and they were also a thousand others according to the vision and need of a particular person or a particular time."

The Book of Ruth is essentially a book of women. Its men may be real, but they are peripheral. Two of them die young, a third—according to this Midrash—

commits suicide, and the fourth, Boaz, produces the impression of having been made to order. Naomi baffles the imagination by her excessive spiritual gifts, Boaz by his excess of propriety. The Men of the Midrash have tried hard to infuse vividness into him; Mrs. Goldin has not, and rightly so. One would think that a man who knew himself to be the predestined ancestor of the Messiah would somehow flash upon the world the radiance of this literally unique election. No; Boaz is a thoroughly upright man, good to count on, good to live with, but terribly hard to write about. It may very well be that the greatest sacrifice God exacts from the sinless is to make them uninteresting, and one sometimes wonders whether Moses would tower as high as he does in our regard if he had not killed the Egyptian and lost his temper with the rock. In any case, it is possible to say that this dullness of Boaz's also belongs, a reflection not on him but on our incorrigibility.

Often, when I think of the Bible and its inexhaustible riches, I recall a passage in Sir Thomas Browne, written nearly three hundred years ago. Said Sir Thomas: " 'Tis too late to be ambitious; the great mutations of the world are acted." It seemed to the physician-philosopher that humanity had done all its worth-while deeds and thought all its worth-while thoughts by the middle of the seventeenth century; and here, in the middle of the twentieth, we stand startled, and sometimes aghast, at the creative prospects that beckon to us. Those who imagine that the lodes of the Bible have been by now completely explored make in our day, in this particular respect, the provincial error that Sir Thomas Browne made in the general respect. I have the feeling that there await us in the field of spiritual biblical discoveries—and these have nothing to do with the parallel but irrelevant fascinations of archeological discovery—developments commensurate with, and more important than, all the other coming intellectual triumphs of man.

MAURICE SAMUEL

I
ELIMELECH

In the days the Judges judged in Israel
(God judge our purposes as He judged theirs!)
Two men of substance lived in Bethlehem,
Upright and canny, Bible millionaires.
Princes they seemed and all men swore by them,
By Boaz, second in his strength to none;
By Elimelech who was blessed as well
With two tall boys, Mahlon and Chilion.
Though decades passed, but Boaz had no son,
God's purpose was to make him ancestor
Of David, of the King:—a prophecy
Boaz received from many a soothsayer
And would have given his very life to be
One half so sure of as the witches were.

Some thirty years these two lived side by side,
Ruling or judging, laying up their wealth
And harvesting in honor from the town.
They were like two tall hills to Bethlehem
And only God (as His wise custom is)
Knew one of them to be a granite stone
And one no other than a heap of sand.
For thirty years God cherished to Himself
His private estimate of Elimelech,
Reluctant, in His way, to bring distress
Down on the faithful head of Naomi,
But waiting neither for her sake nor His:
Waiting, as only God can wait, for time
To bring about the circumstance

And bring to birth the characters
And ripen them in thought, and make the weather,
So that the play can play itself alone.
There came a day, however, in the spring
When God sent out, instead of rains and flowers,
A steadily hot wind that blew for hours.
And Boaz could see famine roll behind
That coursing, merciless, and dry-mouthed wind.
He stood up straighter, called about his men
To check the granaries with last year's growth,
Package the millet, measure out the oats,
Winnow the wheat and weigh the barleycorn
Against what time his hungry folk would come,
Trustful and indigent, to beg their bread.
While Boaz paced his corridor of nights,
Restless, and halfway maddened by the wind,
"I think we are equipped," he told his wife,
"To care for them this summer through the fall;
Then if the rains return to Bethlehem,
We shall lose neither man nor animal."

In one more great establishment that night
They feared the wind as much as it deserved,
For Elimelech was a farmer too.
He had lived through a famine once before
And with a bitter rind of thought recalled
Naomi's shrunken body, and the voice
Of undernourished beggars quacking, "Bread!"
How can a man deny them? Drawing up
His seat within the court, where it was cool,

The man in this wise reasoned with his wife:
"Naomi, Heaven in His righteousness
Claps down a sentence on our fellow men
Who blaspheme Him, and walk on the right hand
Of the heathen-born in their iniquity.
We saw it coming: we exclaimed with God:
'Is this My faithful city, Bethlehem?'
Nevertheless, I prayed that God might pluck
Some more discriminating punishment
Than wind that parches up the very skin
Of just and unjust, foul and merciful,
And may, if retribution fit the sin,
Bring all of us in famine to the dust."
To which Naomi: "Heaven's will is just."

Then Elimelech: "Did I say one word
For you to take as censure of the Lord?
No; my concern is rather to debate
How we may fit us to His purposes,
Not crushed below Him like a worm of the earth,
Not hoping to escape, if ours the guilt
And circumstance of this catastrophe,
Since God can halt us with a finger-nail
If such should be His will. Oh, no, Naomi:
I do but reason inwardly, how best
We may be saved—if God would have us saved
When Sodom burns with evil to the ground—
Like righteous father Abraham, who strode
At summons hastily betwixt the flames.
As God led forth our father's nephew Lot

Into the pasture of a distant land,
So it may be, that by this wind He speaks
To those of us with wit to understand:
'My wrath,' says He, 'goes out against this folk.
I will consume its substance hideously.
Rise up and flee, as fled from Sodom Lot
To Moab's healthy meadows; rise and flee,
You and your wife, your wealth, your family.' "

Then spoke his wife: "If famine comes again
To smite our citizens of Bethlehem,
Whose conduct, trust me, has not been so vain
Nor crimes so frantic as you pictured them,
Would not God's word beseech you to remain
To save His folk whatever way you can?
We have a full sufficiency of grain,
More than is needful for a pious man.
You and your brother Boaz stand as one,
Tall in your fame and equally beloved;
Boaz will scarcely think as you have done,
For he is rock and may not be removed;
But when the people wake to find you gone,
They will despair, as though the earth had moved!"

But Elimelech, biting down his spleen:
"Let's let the rabble seek out Boaz, then!
He has to gain by being generous.
An old man, Boaz, sixty if a day,
And that, Naomi, makes him old enough
To be my father, if he had it in him,

But by the Lord's inscrutable decree
He will not father be to any man.
All moonshine and burnt magic is the talk
Of sir great-grandson king and emperor;
It would be best for Boaz if he put
His mind on this world's business for a spell
Than wait for royal grandsons to arise,
Begot upon a legend by a cloud,
To call their father back before men's eyes.
What though the man should sacrifice his wealth?
The difficult, only begotten grain
Will scarcely feel its separation from
Those cribs of Boaz where it lay so long.
And if all be to no avail, if God
Unleashed this wind to wipe out Israel,
Boaz will sow in vain, but reap in fame:
No man but Boaz could invest so well.
Whichever way you look upon this case
I think it wise of him to spill his strength
Trying to make the dry sands bear again.
I know the people will be better off
That there was once a Boaz in the world,
Whether their death come on them now, or whether
God will relent, and moisten up the weather.
If Boaz had the sons God granted us
He'd find it hard to be magnanimous.
What life has Boaz that it ought not cease?
One decade of a steadily decreased
Responsibility; some helpless weeks
When strangers lift him up or lay him down

And the mind wanders, calling for its son;
Then at the end, I say, there'll be no son
To wipe his face or set the burial stone."

"But if our sons go out of Israel,"
Cried Naomi to him, "I cannot tell
How you imagine you are planning well!

Here in these fields of Bethlehem so far
They have grown straight as other children are,
Neither more pious nor more singular.

But boys of twelve and boys of seventeen
Do not for long remember what has been;
And Moab's pasture-land grows very green.

With what composure can you buy them bread
Ground in the mills of sin and uglihed?
I think the stuff will poison them instead."

Her husband spat. "Where there's no bread at all
There'll be no Torah. Woman, look about!
Where can you come on truth in Bethlehem?
I tell you that this village reeks with sin,
Cloaking it up within a decency
More to be feared, and more insidious
For boys of twelve and boys of seventeen
Than Moab, where the ripe sin sickens us:

28

It is a flaming warrant to the eyes,
Abomination to the ears, and stench
Within the nostrils of the innocent.
Our little boys who mumbled tender-mouthed
'Love ye your neighbors'; 'keep the festivals';
Once they have read in Moab's evil writ
Will know the wrong forever from the right.
You shall prepare them with the world for school:
'My sons, beware! Across the market road
Harlotry saunters in her bright red coat
And silver shoes like bells; whom you shall know
By these same signs forever to forego.'
As for your comfort, I shall build you courts
Richer by far than these in Bethlehem
And wall them round with flower and with vine
And hide them in the hiding of the hills.
There we shall dwell as dwelt our ancestors
To God more dedicate than here among
Ten thousand praying fools who mar our thought
With the deceitful passage of their tongue.
I say this bitter wind was Heaven-sent!"
Exulted Elimelech. So they went.

    When Elimelech quit the Land
    He thought he fled starvation;
    He had no mind to desecrate
    The customs of his nation.

But camping in a pagan place
He did what pagans do:
He broke their bread, he drank their wine,
He tipped their retinue;
And when the great cup came around,
He poured libations too.

Till it was so, his very life
Interpreted the text:
In innocence, in innocence,
Will Israel be vexed;
A Jew that left the Holy Land
Will serve Baalim next.

It happened in the seventh year in Moab
Of Elimelech, after he had thrived
Thanks to a commerce and to a rewarding
Mutual tolerance between his wealth
And the blond princes of the countryside:
So goes the world; when he had raised his house
According to the plan, or splendider,
It came about that Elimelech grew
Increasingly morose. He would not trade,
Withdrew from court and marketplace; and scraped
A rude bare burnt place out behind his lot
To set up sacrifice as was the way
Of Israel, and pray. His was of all
High places the most low. The sycamores
Hid priest and altar. None in Moab knew,

Save for his household, how he sought out God:
Sought, but not found; prayed, and he never heard
Authentic echo of his Hebrew there;
Called to the sky, that after Moab's great
And hideous gold gods seemed far away.
The more he prayed, the further off God went.
Then Elimelech took to sacrifice,
Recklessly burning up firstling and flock,
Great ox and heifer, little goats and lambs;
Whole droves of them refused to summon God.
That long black year Naomi, proper wife,
Ordered the farm and sent to field the slaves.
When Elimelech, late at night, returned,
His hand still slippery with the blood of lambs,
Naomi looked him up and down. She said
Nothing at all. She never said a word.
In silence—not his medium—he battled
Whatever wars broke over him. At first
He thought God insular; but the mere doubt
Of one truth wholly necessary—God
As God of every land—he could not suffer
And cast it with the next sheep to the flames.
As that caught fire the smoke would not rise straight,
Which naturally brought to his recall
A man named Cain. Oh, did the Lord reject
This sacrifice as He rejected Cain's?
But Cain was bloody born, a murderer,
He slew his brother Abel with his hand,
While Elimelech never yet had killed
One soul save cattle. Cattle have no souls

So how could Elimelech kill his brothers?
Be literal. Is Elimelech Cain?
Who sent him forth to wander through the world?
Would wandering make Cain of him, or was
Some base ingredient in the blood the same?
Word had been sent that famine after all
Was not so bad in Judah as one feared:
It was not actually very bad.
This news cheered Elimelech, if a man
So bitterly sorry can admit of cheer:
No Jew, he reassured himself, had died
By reason of that swift departure. None
Had even hungered very much, for Boaz
Made haste to care for all. Boaz redeemed
His brother Elimelech, who was now,
No, not in any sense a murderer.
But, just because of this, though the rains fell
And seasons moved again in Bethelehem,
That sorry Elimelech and his wife
Might not go home: Moab must be their home.
How could a man look Boaz in the face?
And Israel would talk—had talked indeed,
He knew their ilk—why, even at this distance
He heard the things they said in Bethlehem.
So Elimelech rose, and built one day
An altar high as any Moab god's
Cut of the rough undecorated stone,
Where with a wholly unrestrained display,
More like the heathen than like Israel,
He prayed to God. He called the heavens down.

He slit his skirt, he cut his flesh, he crawled
Weakly below the unapproaching God.

So matters stood; and one evening the sons
Of Elimelech brought great news home with them.
As men they prospered, living now in town,
Serving King Eglon as his bodyguard;
They entered with misgivings. Mother would,
They hoped, take word of this sort sensibly,
But father, being partly mad, required
Delicate management. Father appeared
From his—in charity we speak—devotions;
With sour mouth he kissed his sons, while they,
As one would lure a child, spoke gently with him:

MAHLON:
  Father, in all good cheer we come, with news—
  Good news—to reassure you past all doubt
  Your God did not abandon us in Moab
  Nor hide His countenance, as you in saintly
  Overanxiety supposed; with news
  Conclusively to demonstrate God's favor
  And man's goodwill toward this lost family;
  Lastly, with news that shall provide the way
  For you to shrink from trade and live with heaven
  And make your conscience easy, since without
  Further investment on your part you may
  Prosper indeed, and dwell in eminence.

33

ELIMELECH:

Prosper in God, my word has ever been,
Or perish. What's the news?

CHILION:

The King of Moab,
Our royal master Eglon, he whose strength
Throughout Transjordan is the law, has viewed
Your Jewish sons with quite unusual favor;
Though we may here confess the thought of it
Was introduced into his royal mind
To some slight measure by the royal daughters;
A man's mind, even a king's they say, is guided,
Sometimes misguided, by his sons and daughters;
But had we not found favor with the father
He could not countenance his daughters' plans.

ELIMELECH:

Which are?

MAHLON:

Make yourself quieter, dear Father.
Eglon has chosen us to wed his daughters.

ELIMELECH:

Oh, so I feared! Oh, so my heart foretold
As I stepped patiently after you along
This labyrinth of favors and of fathers.
Is it not enough I lent you to the King,
Spared you from harvest and inheritance,

34

Gave my consent, God knows how fearfully,
That you be soldiers in the troops of Moab
As Jewish boys were never wont to be—
For some day they may send you out to slaughter
Your own blood-brethren—soldiers, murderers—

CHILION:

Dear Father, all has been arranged. We pray you
Add your voice to our blessedness, and bless us.
We marry well: the purest blood in Moab.

ELIMELECH:

Speak me no sorrow. Will you be foresworn?
Will you slough off the Lord of Hosts, and haste
To bind you to this heathen He despised:
To join our good blood with the blood of Lot
Who in incestuous intercourse begot
Moab with all its mirth and wickednesses?

CHILION:

You speak of royal blood as if it were
The brine of fishwives. You have seen the maidens
Some years ago at court. You must recall them.
They are as they were then, but quieter.

MAHLON:

Ruth

Is like some slender damsel of fourteen:
I never saw in Israel or Moab
Woman of such a hushed gracefulness!

35

Low in her speech and marvellous in motion,
The dancer tamed.

ELIMELECH:

                    The dancer at what altar?
Profane, idolatrous!

CHILION:

                            Father, do Jews
Monopolize this wide world's decency?

ELIMELECH:

The very tents in Israel, they say,
Call forth a blessing from the passer-by
For that their doors look not into each other,
But modestly, as if with downcast eyes,
Like some unwedded girl in hesitance,
Each tent peeps out across its private fields.
If tents, then how much more so men? And how
Much more so than the men the Jewish women?

MAHLON:

And yet the heathen have their heroines:
Our father Moses married a black woman;
Whereas my Ruth is fair as is God's sun,
More gold than gold is, golden through and
    through
And pure as the refined gold her heart.
What better wife to prove the heroine
Even of Israel?

ELIMELECH:

O miser, miser,
This beauty blinds you. Let you not be led
Astray by beauty in the godless folk!
Not one thing that they own compares with ours,
Neither their camels nor their womankind,
Nor priests nor men, nor fields nor sacrifice.

MAHLON:

There rose a prophet out of Moab once,
As great in God's eyes for the needs of Moab
As Moses was, to speak for Israel.
God's spokesmen both. They call their prophet
    Balaam.

ELIMELECH:

That I should live to hear my sons invoke
The wicked Balaam for their evidence!

MAHLON:

He came and with his mighty blessing blessed
All Israel.

ELIMELECH:

Mahlon, he came to curse:
God was too strong for him, God overpoured
The thought of curse with words of benison:
How goodly are thy tents, O Israel—
O heart, O Elimelech, break!

CHILION:

Your God
Chose Balaam for His fitting instrument
And spoke through him, and to him it may be,
Rank pagan though he was—

ELIMELECH:

I tell you, cease!
Obstinate asses! Balaam me no more!

CHILION:

Father, forgive me. Truly I'd no thought
But to persuade you gently as a mother.

ELIMELECH:

Persuade me you cannot, in any wise,
If I must yield me to such purposes.
What place did Balaam bless? It was not Moab.
You in your turn, my sons, must pardon me:
It is so long since you were gone from home
And I of late have been preoccupied;
It is as though I turned my back, and found
Looking again, my boys had leapt to manhood;
You are of age to marry, you do right
To cast about you for a fitting wife,
And I your father, long before this season,
Ought to have brought you back to Bethlehem.
Our mission here is finished. Let us go,
Let us go home once more, where you may wive
Congenial daughters of our Jewish parents,

38

Neither too ripe nor too luxurious.
No maid in Bethlehem will hesitate
To marry indeed men so well placed as you.
Then travel up like Jacob to the Land
Seeking the wives of your inheritance.

CHILION:

If we marry in Israel, we marry milkmaids
Instead of princesses.

MAHLON:

                               Oh, if we marry
In Israel or Judah, we will take
Some stranger to be mother of our children
Rather than Ruth.

CHILION:

                      We never learned the Hebrew
Love-words to speak with women such as these.

MAHLON:

Father, forget not we have lived in Moab
The best part of our lives; that we are Moab
In speech, in clothes, in thoughts, in all but spirit.
Do not believe that we have worshipped idols:
No, our religion is our Jewishness
Which we have cherished in all purity,
Not tricked out with the long-archaic customs
Of what they did one time in Israel;
Not limited by place or priest or fetish:
Our Jewish God goes with us everywhere.

CHILION:

>We have honored all the festivals and fasted
>On the days we are told to fast; and watched our
>>diet.

MAHLON:

>Don't think our being Jewish played no part
>In the affections of our princesses.
>There's something terribly dark and Oriental,
>Ruth says, about my Jewish way of thinking . . .

CHILION:

>Besides, the word goes out Jews make good
>>husbands,
>And princesses ought to make us good wives.

ELIMELECH:

>Oh, well were you named Chilion, the Destroyed,
>And Mahlon, who was Blotted out from living!
>Men drank in Bethlehem, where you were named,
>The winecup of the Covenant; they drained
>Your health, they brought my condemned sons
>>to me
>With the voice of music and congratulation.
>Oh, why was Boaz sent a prophecy
>While I had none?

CHILION:

>>   Return, sad heart, return;
>Go back to Bethlehem where you were born,
>Where the men talk as you would want them to

40

And worship in the way you always wanted to:
Count out your gold, sell out your property,
And to the barleyfields of your tradition,
Now being old, return.

ELIMELECH:

                              And you?

MAHLON:

                                    Your sons
Mahlon and Chilion have come of age
To make their choice. We will remain in Moab,
Marry our princesses, and lead such lives
As shall, by reason of their decency,
Silence these arguments.

ELIMELECH:

                              And yet you speak
To your old father touching his return.
Shall I go back to Bethlehem, with boast
Of cunning little pagan grandchildren
Who mount my knee and with their earliest chirp
Render the invocation to Astarte?
Who name Baalim long before they lisp
The word for grandpapa? Or will your mother,
This Naomi, conceive me other children
To make atonement for your double loss?
My sons, you sentence us to a perpetual
Banishment.

MAHLON:

It grieves us. Yet you brought
Your sons from Bethlehem when they were boys,
And then I felt some twinges of regret,
Some thought of wheatfields gone, of friends, of women
That had begun to look my way; while Chilion
Mourned outright for his playmates lost, and vowed
That with our Heaven's help he would not thrive
Out here in Moab of the wildernesses.
We taught ourselves how not to think, or grieve,
And not to count on going back, since you
So obviously had set your will against it.

ELIMELECH:

I brought you out of Bethlehem to save you
From a great famine, all ways hideous:
This is the way you thank me.

CHILION:

No one starved
That year in Bethlehem. Not even Boaz.

ELIMELECH:

A Jew, my sons, must take into account,
On the part of sinner or of saint, intention;
And if I have sinned, as it seems to me
At times like this, when my sons rise against me,
I pray you judge me by my full intent:
Which was, to save four lives in Israel,

Protect my seed, and harvest my succession.
Come, let us talk together, not with wrath,
Not with impatience, not with emphasis,
Let us speak very calmly, as befits
A Jewish parent counselling his sons
Out of his greater wisdom, with his knowledge
Of life in two lands that may well evade you.
My sons, believe me, marriages like these
In Jewry's history, and in the life
Of every Jew reckless enough to risk them,
Have not been known to bring them satisfaction.
They are cursed with such a great curse as you
    know not:
Heaven will not permit Himself to be
Openly flouted even by the Jew
Whom exile tainted. Moab or no Moab,
Your inmost natures, Chilion and Mahlon,
Are Jewish: I begot them so myself;
And howsoever you will stubbornly temper
Your Jewish natures in the fires of freedom,
Such freedom was not meant for us, my boys:
We thrive best in the bondage of the Lord.
Strange illnesses will strike at your heart's root,
And you shall sicken with a foul disease;
Your wives will neither of them know you then
For they their whole lives long found health in
    freedom.
Despite their loves, though they might want to
    do so
They cannot learn, their highnesses your wives,
Which way to treat this fever so to cure it.

43

They take no portion in our heritage.
I think God did not mean for us to mix
Without a scruple with the pagan nations;
I scarcely hope your son, my grandson, can
Discover in his mangled self the strength
For manhood either as a Jew or pagan.

MAHLON:

Manasseh and Ephraim were, dear Father,
Halfbreeds themselves; a tribe in Israel
Or halftribe to this day. My little sons
Will please me best by being like Ephraim,
As the old blessing goes, or Manasseh.

ELIMELECH:

Ah, Lord my God, how these wild sons of mine
Pervert the very words of blessing on them!
Do not forget it, though You recognize
Their fathers' blood in this stiffneckedness.
Shall I obey, dear Lord? I'll not obey.
Shall I give them my fatherly consent?
I will not give them my consent. Why, I'll
In every manner thwart them and prevent them!
Both of my sons. Both, both to be wed.
Not in my lifetime, by the Name of God!
Some curse I'll find to curse them, as I live,
And break apart their Jewish-planted pride!

That night Naomi's husband left their bed,
He climbed his altar of the rough-hewn stone,
Cast himself bodily down from it, and died.

II
NAOMI

"And Mahlon and Chilion," our sources read,
"Died, both of them": but no book tells us why:
Whether, as the Midrashic texts imply,
They were made victims of their father's greed,
And his sin fell upon their generation
And his atonement equally was theirs;
As, being Jews, they naturally stood heirs
To his deserts (our first interpretation).

Though Moab would have told you otherwise:
Their outlook for long life could not be worse;
For, since his marriage, each man had to live
Under the shadow of a dying curse,
And this would leave them both (in Moab's eyes)
No safer than the guiltiest fugitive.

Or we might say: both sons inherited
Their father's shortcomings; their father knew
What they were and were not, what they must do,
And when they balked, what consequence they
   merited.
Those princesses they valued so, they got—
Orpah and Ruth, as pagan as the day—
Who overmatched them, meaning not to slay,
But just to uninhibit them somewhat.

One other (and our last) interpretation;
This too the twentieth century might provide,
Thinking of chance, the accidental twist:

Two men there lived in Moab, but they died
Of some disease peculiar to their nation
That neither one had virtue to resist.

In spice-bark and in laurel and in myrrh,
With keening and the fatal sound of bells,
With all the arts a heathen culture knows
Of how to elegize, how to embalm,
How to encase in brightly handled gold
The happily indifferent corpse; with all
The pomp a royal setting would require,
Moab, its princes and authorities
Laid two young Jews inside their grave to rest
Neither the gold, nor incense, nor the bells
Comforted Ruth and Orpah in the least.
It was as though a foreign-born procession
Practised a triumph in familiar streets.
They looked in vain to Eglon, to his guards,
His men-in-waiting, and his woman slaves,
His mourners paid to mourn, his undertakers,
And every eye they saw was clear and blue
Like the sky waiting for a rain to cease.
They looked to right, to left; then up the street
They saw a woman coming all in grey,
Barefooted, with a bundle on her back,
And in their hearts the princesses were glad
To see at last the sign of so much grief.
For once they knew Naomi—knew her mind,
Darkness and all; and they two came to meet her,

Threw out their arms around her neck, and wailed,
All three together, in the village court.
The gala princesses, the broken Jew
Mourned with one word and one dark binding
thought.

And then Naomi moved apart, and dropped
Her bundle to the road, and squatted on it.
Her straightness totally took leave of her;
And, as her daughters knelt by her in grief,
Thus raising up her voice, Naomi wept:

"I am a woman whom the Lord has cursed;
Cursed are all who ever dwelled with me.
All that I took into my hand to do
The Lord has brought it to calamity.

On the day my husband rode from Israel
I did oppose it, and my husband perished;
I had his curse from him, or he had mine,
One of us led into destruction.
On the day my sons made public their decision
To marry wives and plant themselves in Moab
I dared not challenge it, I said and trembled,
That way is cursed: the other way, Naomi!
Oh, this time you must take the other way!
Look to their safety, make them prosperous
With one god or another, say no word.
When lo, because they stayed, my two sons perished:
It may be that of my consent they died!

And God repeatedly warned us, had we ears
To hearken, eyes to look upon the Lord.
What but a warning was my Elimelech's
Madness and eventual suicide?
The loss of asses, oxen, camels, and
At last these young lives lingering into death?
The Lord God does not state a death-warrant
All in one breath, or with one final word:
He speaks, and waits; He speaks and waits once more
And only on the wholly deaf will pour
His unreprieved, His thunderous retribution.

There is no way to double back this curse:
I would outrun it, but it follows after.
Let it then strike me down in Israel,
In Bethlehem, on the Judaean road;
In whatsoever Hebrew town it finds me
I think that I can bear it better there.
My daughters, tell me how to comfort you.
To the dead you were at all times kind. Because
Of you alone they both found burial
Not without honor, though of such rude nature
As never Jew in his right mind would suffer.
When was a Jew decked out in spikenard
And what Jew wore tiaras when he died?
Nevertheless, I know your hearts, I know
The love you bore my sons, and for your sakes
More than my own I grieve. Oh princesses,
I cannot counsel you. I cannot bless.

I pray that Moab somehow give you wisdom
And that your father's gods bring happiness."

With that Naomi kissed them, raised her pack,
And turned along the dusty road to Judah,
Down which, with donkeys and with gold, she
    came—
She and her husband and her two tall sons—
In one month it would be ten years ago.
Behind her went her daughters. When she saw
That they still followed her, Naomi spoke
Once more to them, with rising urgency:
"My daughters, that are nobly born in Moab,
Why would you follow me?" And still they came
And each one took Naomi by an arm
Keeping firm step with her upon the dust.
"I am a bitter woman, have no sons,
Will have none, and should have no more. Return!
I am a salt, abandoned sea, I lie
Too deep for you; I would not have you with me
If at a word I could. I give to man,
To woman and to child, no kind refreshment
But lightlessness at all times of the day,
So I beseech you not to follow me."
The two girls bent their heads, and followed her.
"If you will not credit my word, and for
Your own sakes go, then for Naomi's sake
I pray you flee the curse that cleaves to me!
I do not want to kill another soul

51

Either in Moab or in Israel!"
Then as they walked, Ruth turned to her and spoke.

"The proof of blessing rests upon the blessed
Just as a curse is known by its destruction.
Suppose your power to curse has been exhausted
In Moab, on your two sons and your husband
(If truly it was you who bore disaster,
But that I challenge); yet suppose you squandered
The fatal and involuntary power
On Elimelech, Mahlon, Chilion;
Whence will you draw the further strength to curse?
And who gave you authority to curse?
All curses strike but by permission.
After such catastrophic pouring forth
As you describe, not one drop should be left you,
Not even bitter drops; but deep below you
I hear a rushing of new waters from
The wells that wait there of salvation.
Because of you, I hear this. For my part
I have consistently experienced
A benediction when I came to you;
The thoughts that you engendered in me pushed
Like little plants that break the rock apart.
Consider: I had stood for several years
Like some great statue hammered up in gold,
Encased, and shuttered; when I saw your face
The spiral round me split; and I looked out
To see—I cannot tell you what I saw.
I cannot focus clearly yet; I cannot

Put you within the limits of a word.
But this I know of you: I saw no curse.
You say my mother is a bitter woman,
Salty and sulphurous; but I bear witness
To me you were like musk or lavender,
Your spice has from the first gone to my head.
How shall a costly fragrance be dispersed
While it is stocked? How many people know
The flask of balsam till it be unstopped
And shaken out across the countryside?
And how shall God bring blessing through Naomi
By treasuring her up in Bethlehem?

You say the Lord has cursed you; that may be.
But if this God of yours works lovingly
He does not want His curses to be spread,
But gathers them together on one head
And strikes that down, and strikes that wholly down.
He does not send it to infect a town,
Nor is the bearer of His curses sent
To bring disaster on the innocent.
No, blessing, blessing, was what your God meant.
Why did He send you forth? A miracle!
The purposes of God were merciful;
He had hid many blessings in your load
For you to scatter out upon the road.
And so they fall on willing soil, like seed
The ready plants let fly; and so they breed
And grow, and rise, and flourish till this hour.
Know by our loves, your blessing came to flower."

To whom Naomi: "Kind and courteous
It is on your part, Ruth, to comfort me
Where you have greater need for comforting;
And I am all the more in debt to you
That for my sake you quit your idiom,
Placing your gentle words in my God's mouth,
With the intent to soften harsh Naomi
And, after dire plagues, leave her in peace.
It is a long time since I thought of God,
Or when I did, I thought of the Avenger
And that did violence to His dual nature.
It is uncanny in you how you know
That the Lord punishes, and He forgives;
Breaks, and makes whole again; and resurrects;
Have you such traits in your gold Baalim?
You might have made a very subtle Jew.
However, Ruth, I beg you pardon me:
No dialectic does me any good;
To all the world beside, my God may be
A helpmate and a consolation;
But He has for a decade been to me
Inimical, and a neglectful God;
He cast me off His altar, and He spurned
Me as the remnants of the sacrifice
That His great fire had not wholly burned."

Then Orpah spoke for the first time. "If God
Be all that you have said, both mean and great,
And for no sin nor slipping on your part
Withdrew from you and left you desolate;
And piled down plagues upon your kindly head,

And this not for a day, not for a year,
But ten long years of exile and of dread
With ruin showing every hour more clear;
So that the while your sons approached the throne
All you could think of was the punishment
Of little sins a later time made known
And Heaven chastised to His heart's content,
And there you sat, unfriended and alone,
And not a single soul knew what you meant:

What kind of God is He? Our Baalim
Are this one fair, and that one ominous;
I cannot in a word imagine Him
Who with one body must be all to us:
Do you propitiate Him, or adore?
Do you bring Him your virgins, or firstfruits?
Do you with forehead knock against the floor
Or sing His praises to the sound of lutes?
We have in Moab too some arrogant
Unfriendly gods: they teem throughout the East;
We bring them every feast-day what they want,
Whether the service of a man or beast;
But we would likewise be both plagued and gaunt
Had we let those Baalim rule the feast."

Naomi kissed her. "Orpah, turn aside!
You ought not dabble in such speculations:
The kernels of religious thought reside
Neither in Orpah's heart nor in her nation's;
A darkened mind might be the end of it

If you should force yourself to my conclusion;
Like yours, so was my husband's mind unfit
For heavenly things, that brought him to confusion:

Wife of my Chilion, Orpah, go your ways;
I am returning to my own far country,
Where we greet foreigners with scanty praise
And treat idolators with some effrontery;
And it were well for Ruth to go with you
Back to the atmosphere you always knew.

What can I give you, girl? I am rock-poor,
I cannot dress you, cannot shelter you;
You will be stoned as an idolator
Or taken coolly when you turn a Jew;
Our tongue is difficult, our very air
Is dryer, and our dew is not your dew;
You will not find in Judah anywhere
The courtliness you are accustomed to."

Then Orpah kissed her mother, and shed four—
Four little tears she shed, for Chilion's sake;
And turned about reluctantly, to take
The road to Moab, to her father's door;
But Ruth went on, her eyes like some gold lake,
Holding Naomi's elbow, as before.

"You were too harsh with Orpah," Ruth declared.
"Had you but coaxed her as she dared you to
She might have gone the difficult way with you."

"We are forbidden bribery, my Ruth,"
Replied Naomi, marching steadily now
Down a curve of white, ill-populated hills,
"Since only those who come with extreme love
For heaven and heavenly things, and love of God,
Are welcome to be Jews."

                       "What kind of welcome?"

"Beloved are proselytes before the Lord."

"Naomi, Mother, will you make my soul,
Will you become my mother in all truth?"

"I am afraid, Ruth. I foretold this not,
Nor am I worthy of the power to do it."

"Is this your welcome to the proselyte?"

"No, Ruth, be warned! A curse is on us, Ruth,
You must not join us till you hear of it.
The Lord said to our father Abraham
In the first days of our covenant with Him:
'Since man will sin, and Jews are no exception,
I offer you one choice: Say, shall I smite
Your offspring with the whitest fires of hell,
Or shall I subject them to alien rule
And let the stranger do what hell would do?'
All day our father measured and compared,
Wavering now to one course, now the other,
Till God's voice severed his predicament.

'How long,' cried God, 'will you deliberate?
Commit yourself! and with My guidance choose
Rather than hell of Mine, the alien rule!'
Abraham chose: his choice hangs over us.
Did I beweep, some hours back, my curse?
Set up my flimsy, custom-tailored curse
Next to the great black tent of Abraham!
Ruth, can the daughter of a king conceive
What it is like to be an outcast people?
Lowly and bowed and lowest of all peoples,
And sickness, and chastisements come on them;
They have no earth to be a burial place,
They practise plaints and mitzvot in a cave,
And when they bind tefillin they are lashed,
And put to death for circumcision;
In their own land, for their own laws, are slain:
What does it matter who the stranger be
So long as he shall have more strength than we?
O Ruth, my Ruth, while you can do so, flee!"

"Entreat me not to leave you, dearest heart,
Or to return from following after you.
I'll have the blessing; let me bear your curse;
Sin not against me, I would rightly share
Your suffering."

                          "Then do you know our laws?
A pagan woman is exempt from them
Save for the larger laws of decency:
These I am confident you would observe
In Bethlehem or Moab: basic laws

Not to blaspheme, or rob, or kill, or live
Either in incest or adultery;
A Moabitish princess can remain
Well on the safe side of such laws as these
And undisturbed may live, and at her death
Sleep in a white, perpetual white sleep."

"But if I were a Jew?"

      "A Jewish woman
For any one of three infringements, shall
Meet death in childbirth; and their full detail
Would take a day for me to specify:
If she forget to light the Sabbath lamps,
Or will not guard her monthly purity
With ritual bath and with all due restraint,
Or even if one Friday she forgot
While kneading Sabbath twists, to pinch a piece
And cast it in the fire for sacrifice,
For that minute omission, she may die
A woman's frightful death."

       "Is it the same

For men?"

    "Well for you you are not a man!
There's circumcision, and the laws of prayer,
The law of tithes, and the forgotten sheaf,
And the corner we must leave to feed the poor;
The laws of slaughter and inheritance,

59

Of foods permitted, and of foods unclean,
And heavy tomes beside, concerning which
I shall enlighten you along the road:
Each one of these, not civil law alone,
Not penance rotting in the lawyer's codes;
But each one of the texture and design
Of Jewish life and our salvation.
Do you still want to come along with me,
To stifle up your pretty pagan soul
In the complex of our legality?"

"Dear Mother, whither you shall go I go."

"A Jewish daughter, Ruth, will never go
To drunken theatres or circuses
Or any pagan show."

                                                       "Whither you go
I go."

                                     "A Jewish daughter will not dwell
In a house where they have not put up mezuzas
On every door."

                                        "Where you shall dwell I dwell."

"You must eradicate idolatry
Within yourself: we have one God, one Law;
Our Torah is our one word of command,
And the eternal God is our one God."

60

"I am not worthy of these obligations;
Yet if you will permit me, Naomi,
I would accept your people for my people,
And I would want your God to be my God."

"In the name of Him who spoke, and called this
    world
To being: I accept you, Ruth. Look there!
Those are our hills, the lower ones; and there,
Across a little stream that we call Jordan,
Is your new life: you stand on alien soil:
Up there lies Israel, down here your past;
On the far bank you will begin again.
What more appropriate water could you find
To bathe in, and by that act to become
In every act and privilege a Jew,
Than the stream that separated me from you?
Forgive me if I sought to frighten you:
If I did this, it was that your reward
And merit be the greater to the Lord.
See, we have come to Jordan's pebbled stream:
My Ruth, my proselyte! Immerse thyself."

My God is this world's King:
Before aught else He was:
He was my root and cause
And now my flowering:
My God is this world's King.

61

And all our motions cease
Yet not His dignity:
He was, He is, and He
Will ever be, in peace,
And all our motions cease.

My gracious God is One,
Wherefore His sovereignty
Can never cease to be
And never was begun:
My gracious God is One.

My spirit meekly lies
Both waking and asleep
In His unfailing keep:
Beneath His watchful eyes
My spirit meekly lies.

Then let the Lord but take
My spirit in His hand!
My indecision and
My terror and heartbreak
Then let the Lord but take!

I yield to Heaven here
My body with my spirit,
So I may disinherit
The body of this fear:
Lord God, I will not fear!
I yield to Heaven here.

This was the way they entered Bethlehem:
First went the dusty road ahead of them
And every time that Ruth looked over her
Shoulder the road behind seemed dustier.
Within the gate they heard a ram's horn call,
For it was on the eve of Festival.

Two beggar women entered Bethlehem:
Like tired rags their dresses hung from them;
Long-bosomed matrons, whom she knew as maids,
Addressed Naomi with incredulous gaze
And well-intentioned heads popped out of windows
To see with their own eyes the havoc sin does.

Conversion like a garment many-grooved
Clung fair about Ruth's body as she moved,
Swung from her hair, and swirled against her knee;
Far less ashamed she stood than Naomi;
Her eyes had little candles lit in them:
This was the way they entered Bethlehem.

Of four that fled to Moab
From God's extensive wrath,
The woman by herself returns
Along the self-same path.

O greater shame than if she came
Alone and greatly withered
A daughter of the heathen walks
Provocatively with her.

This is the cleanest instance
Of Heaven's punishment:
Alone on foot Naomi comes
But litter-borne she went.

Is this Naomi, clad in rags
And barefoot by the road?
Is this Naomi who went out
Extravagantly clothed?

Her husband rots in cursed soil
Because the man transgressed:
Call her no more Naomi,
But Marah, bitterness.

Her two tall sons she buried
Beside a pagan brook:
Naomi was the sacrifice
That Heaven overlooked.

III
BOAZ

What strength might men desire
And not expect to find
In Boaz man of Bethlehem, the prince
For all who sought him out in confidence;
Aristocrat, but rightful judging mind
Quick to express what common folk require,
And in the harvest too
More to be trusted than the evening dew,
With grain for feastdays and with grain for dearth,
Till it was said
Seek yonder, ask at Boaz's house for bread,
For he hath cast a blessing on the earth.
Kinsman of Elimelech, yet no fool
To quit his people when he most should rule
And strike such terror into Israel:
Oh, not so Boaz: firm he stood
When all else fell.

And Boaz might acknowledge, if he would,
That power, under God, comes less from strength
Than the extreme imaginings of thrift;
However, then as now, the folk preferred
To think of strength as favor or as gift
Than as the compensation wrung at length
Out of the insane patience of a miser:
No eye saw Boaz, and no rumor heard,
And no one was the wiser
The while he sat awake of nights, and numbered
Pennies of strength like grains of wheat or corn.
Threescore and ten the years since he was born;

How many more years may a man expect
Undimmed virility,
To hold himself in arrogance erect
And be within him what he seems to be?

Was all this thrift but for the sake
Of those in Bethlehem
Or for Another's sake, *kiddush ha-shem*,
That Boaz constantly
Counted his years, both sleeping and awake,
And half in supplication, half in rage,
Struck out to still the subtlest powers that be:
The draining, and the impotence of age.
We know that God loved Boaz, old and young;
That with the folk his honor rests secure,
That even at the heart, this man was pure.
Some other thought—some legend on the tongue
(Words are the strongest) would not let him rest,
Or sip great age as mariners their drink,
Or drop his bold head idly on his breast,
Let his eye wander, let his thoughts not think;
Oh, rest assured,
So Boaz might have done!
Had not (along some alleyway) he heard
School children chant the song about his son.

Men might have said, this life had been achieved.
Had Boaz died
Childless at seventy, they could have grieved
From Bethlehem across the countryside

For this their judge, like God Himself in faith;
And found the man accomplished in his death
And the whole world not overly bereaved.
While twice three generations would remember
The name, the time, the measure of his splendor.
And some man's son, with barren Boaz dead
Would have judged Israel in Boaz's stead.
One man alone had faith in what was fated:
"Messiah son of Boaz." Boaz waited.
He would not die nor age nor change before
His part was played. Boaz the prince could wait.
His future was to be an ancestor;
And not through his fault would it come too late.

How deviously God moves
To bring fulfilment after trial
And indirection, to the man He loves!
For fifty years, Boaz had had a wife
Whom God had set like Hagar at his side
To comfort him the while
Ruth ripened down in Moab, and the life
Of Mahlon had been wasted, and he died.
This wife of Boaz bore no child. The day
Naomi came with Ruth to Bethlehem,
Worn out with years, the woman passed away
So that her funeral first welcomed them.
And Boaz mourned, and rose, and then through tears
Spoke with the Holy One blessed be He,
Most long and earnestly,
Of all his fears

Concerning what was prophesied
And what he felt must be.
Thus Boaz, as he sacrificed one black unblemished
ram,
With bitter tact reminded God of Father Abraham.

"Lord God: I scarcely need to speak at length
To state my private claims upon your strength.
What my worth is You know; we know your
strength
Throughout this land of yours its breadth and
length

In years of planting, harvest, and of seed
I sowed the necessary grain to feed
Your cattle and your people. Lo, they feed!
Now let your servant also sow his seed.

Look down upon your subject, O my King.
I have not crossed your will in any thing
Concerning which our Sages say this thing:
The son of his son's son shall be the king!

Good Father, who the entire earth hast fathered,
My Harvester, grant that my seed be gathered.
Then, if You will, let Boaz's life be gathered
And let me never see the son I fathered.

You know my child curled downward in the
womb
And his son's son You go with to the tomb;

You see my death and You have set my tomb.
You know which womb is the predestined
   womb."

When they were in the town a month or so
Ruth told Naomi: "This will never do!
I'd rather chill all winter in a hut
Than listen to suchlike commiseration
From cousin this and great-granduncle that:
Poverty I can face, not patronage.
All day and every day the passersby
Accuse us with how miserable we are
And say what great respect they feel for God
Seeing Naomi in these circumstances.
I am tired of hearing of the wrath of God,
I weary of divine recompensation;
They have waved the hand of Heaven in our faces
Too often in these thirty days for me
To acknowledge with a bow its salutation.
They sigh, 'Is this Naomi!' till you look
The secondhanded thing they take you for.
Let me go out to glean as poor girls do:
We need at least not eat out of their hand.
Bide here, and greet your brethren cheerily.
Let not an aunt among them weep for you
More than is strictly necessary. Say,
'My daughter Ruth is in the fields today;
She will fetch home enough to feed us both!'"

Naomi did not tell Ruth where to go:
Naomi left that detail to the Lord
Who weaves up marriages with His right hand
In heaven, where our changing souls are made,
And knots this life to that with colored thread.
Some say a flying angel led Ruth on,
Some say there was in Bethlehem but one
Great field, which she was bound to fall upon;
Be that as it may, Ruth threw her cloak about her,
And turning right, then left, then up a lane,
She saw to one side gleaners in a fair
Ripe field of barley, so she ventured in.

>Shall the princess, shall the daughter
>Of a proud profane tradition
>Hold her head the least bit lower
>Than befits the King's position?
>Shall she muddy her complexion
>Or her walk make crookeder
>Because the men of Moab
>Drop work to look at her?
>Oh, Orpah was a princess
>That knew how men behave,
>Yet when she left Naomi
>She took what Moab gave:
>A man for every step, they say:
>Look over there, where lieth
>The princess in a gutter-lane
>Conceiving Prince Goliath.
>While Ruth, her sweeter sister

Who longed for Israel,
Found out that men who speak with God
Seek other things as well.
Now ought a convert squint or limp
When Hebrews find her fair?
Ruth cast a veil across her face,
A scarf about her hair,
And moved along so secretly
She scarcely stirred the air.
And still the men looked after her:
They seemed to guess the shape
Of that most disturbing woman
In a grass-grey cape.

The following day the barley shone with gold
And spun about like brightness in a row;
Accustomed reapers went where they were told,
Stripped down the barleyheads, but not too low;
Then gleaners scurried after them, some bold,
Some humble, to crop up their residue;
And Boaz on his dais felt less old
Than since his wife's death he was wont to do:
Only his eyes played tricks on him. They showed
His barley wandering from place to place,
One cluster in particular, that glowed
With quite unbarleylike richness and grace,
Till as the gold came wavering up the road
It was a woman; and he saw Ruth's face.

His first thought was: How might this woman be
Closely akin to me?—his next, to watch
Her manner and her walk most carefully,
And he saw how the reapers let her catch
The full stalk, or let drop before her three
Or four ripe heads; or how the men would fetch
Water for Ruth; he saw incredulously
How she was tended by the lowliest wretch.
He saw her cloak of some green stuff like grass
And her bare toes, how peacefully they moved,
And her bright hair, like yellow lines of glass,
And all the man took note of, he approved.
He saw how unlike Bethlehem she was:
He saw the pagan Ruth Naomi loved.

"What woman is this woman
With my petitioners?
There's not a maid among them
Of courtesy like hers!
                    They wink the eye
                    And they shake the hip
                    They heave a sigh
                    At my widowership;
                    They hike the skirt
                    And they bare the thighs
                    And they show famine
                    In their eyes;
But this new woman gleans with them for hours
Like a queen's daughter gathering in her flowers!"

"My Lord, the girl is Ruth,
Naomi's daughter."

"Is it so in truth?
By my faith, she is less pagan than I thought her.
Suppose you knew
No better, would you not think Ruth the Jew?
   My other gleaners catch up every grain,
   Ruth leaves on the barleystalk as much again;
   They pluck their portions out between the
     sheaves,
   Ruth is content with what the reaper leaves;
   My women bend down lower than is meet,
   But when Ruth sits, she covers up her feet;
   They jest among the reapers in the dell,
   Ruth creeps all hushed in her little shell:
       Naomi, bitter Naomi,
       You taught your daughter well!

This shall be Boaz's word concerning her:
Let me not hear of one Jew spurning her,
Nor shall you grant her less grain than her due
On the pretext she was not born a Jew;
Reproach her not; let ever more grain fall
For Ruth is scrupulous, she will recall
The laws of gleaning, and will not take all;
Finally, let none rebuke her here:
I'll countenance no unholy jest, no leer,
No man molest with so much as a wink
The virtuous woman when she goes to drink;

It would not do, when Ruth has come so far,
For her to learn what men of the earth we are.
But at the noon hour, when the work stands still,
Have her approach my dais, if she will,
That by my maidens she may eat her fill."

Said the maidens and the mothers of the maidens
And the widows with their ten good years ahead:
May the Lord provide a suitor for each woman born
    in Judah
When its prince prefers a pagan girl instead!

Have you ever seen the like of it, my sister?
Prince Boaz scarcely knows that we exist.
Regardless of his danger, he revolves around the
    stranger,
Till the stranger has to beg him to desist.

Did you see the burial he gave her husband?
Can you cherish any doubt of his intention?
Do you note the wheat and barley and the way they
    stop and parley
And the sundry little tokens I could mention?

Do you hear the way she sings about her gleaning?
Mistake me not, I bear the girl no grudge;
But I will say I don't know as it would not be best
    for Boaz
To remember Samson also was a judge.

76

With extraordinary wrath
Prince Boaz paced his lands;
He scowled upon his reapers
And he criticized his hands.

"Word comes to us of whoring
Within these fields of late;
We know not who the Jew can be
So reckless of his fate.

But whoso we convict of it
When inquiries are made
We banish out of Bethlehem
Forevermore," he said.

"On this account," said Boaz,
"Tonight I mean to lie
With you men on the threshing-floor
Under an open sky.

Is this place Israel," he cried,
"Or Moab, or Beth-Peor?"
So Boaz came himself to lie
Upon the threshing-floor.

And Naomi said to Ruth, "How long, my Ruth,
Can you and Boaz play your little game?
Lo, it is seven weeks since the crop began
And seven weeks Ruth has gone out harvesting.
Is not Prince Boaz of our kinsmen, whose

Maidens you daily follow to the fields?
Shall I not seek your rest, and ascertain
That it be well with you and well with me?
Behold, the harvesting is over and done,
Tonight they winnow wheat on the threshing-floor.
Rise up, my daughter; rise, adorn yourself,
Put Sabbath raiment on, undo your hair
And some sweet scent apply to garment's hem
Such as my sons desired you wear for them.
Then cautiously, when the night's work is done
And revelry drops silent, creep about
To where, among his reapers, Boaz sleeps.
Uncover his feet, my daughter; crouch down there;
Let Boaz tell you what you ought to do.
I was too young by twenty years to be
This Boaz's wife; now let Naomi try
To make a fitting mother for him." Ruth
Laughed with delight, full princess that she was,
And her eyes glittered like the points of a crown
To think she had quit Moab, and become
A pious woman and a proselyte
And all this way to Bethlehem had come
To play a trick so typically Moabite.
She robed herself in kirtle soft and light
With little flecks of crimson in its weave
And she released her gold hair braid by braid.
Then over all she cast a widow's cape,
Lest revelers see her in the darkened court.
Ruth went down to the fields right merrily.
The night was dark, its moon not yet come up,

And the harvest, after many weeks, complete.
In the lanes, in the warm land, two by two the youth
Of Bethlehem yet roved the meadows sweet.
Naomi's voice made music for Ruth's feet:
"My merits will accompany you, Ruth."

Several steps beyond his laborers
Boaz laid ready couch and covering,
Stretched himself out, and upwards of an hour
He lay on guard, but afterwards he slept.
That night the moon rose late. As Boaz dreamed,
A dozen Ruths skimmed past him single-file,
Each like that Ruth who graced the barley-rows,
But each one bolder than the living Ruth.
As the eleventh of them came abreast
And on the coverlet shook out her braids,
Boaz the proud, who never begged before,
Cried on her mercy! Twelfth Ruth mimicked him:
"Mercy, my Lord? Right mercy comes from God,
After whose footsteps I have walked of late,
But if you prettily ask me, I might grant
One single drop, to cool you of your pain;
Two, but the man in you would wake again;
Three, or a hundred; mercy down might rain
And Boaz drink it all, and drink in vain.
Mercy might rock before you like a pool,
But you sit flaming on the nearby bank.
For such a frenzy as the Lord hath given
His trusty servant, and the world's great fool,
Sweet gentleman, you have yourself to thank."

79

At that, Ruth whirled about, and Boaz woke,
Who with a seventy year accumulation
Of fury cursed his own imagination.
Had he stored seed through half a century
To spill it in a dream upon a slut?
What of the legend? God had promised him
Son of his flesh: begot upon what woman?
Would such a convert be God's messenger?
Was this an omen, or the shades of sin?
He shut his eyes in pain, and on the spot
Up nodded Ruth, the thirteenth of her line,
Discreet yet mocking, brief yet eloquent.
"Greetings, my sometime master!" With what wit
Her toying left him, Boaz thrust her off,
Woke with huge effort and with some regret
And sombrely lay staring at the night.
About him blackness every which way turned
And fire burned within him, and beneath;
And wheatfields overheard him when he groaned
"Judge no man till the moment of his death!"

Now Boaz slept, a heavy, drunken sleep
And when he woke again it was to find
The body of a woman at his feet.
She was warm, and something silk was over her;
Tense, but not overly tense as Boaz was
Who guessed, from the fragrance, from the softness, from
His intuition who the woman was.
And his one thought became

That this should be no dream; or, being one,
He would speak softly that he might not wake.
"Who art thou?" he called out, in a mere shell
Of his man's voice. "Art thou spirit or woman?"
"I am a woman." "Maid or married woman?"
"I am a maid." "Are thou clean or unclean?"
Then she thought, "I am in a purer state
Than you are now, my lord; I need not wait
Until tomorrow eve to be made clean";
And said, "I am clean." A woman, purest of women,
Lay at his feet, and he could feel her breathe;
And again he said, "Who art thou?" and she sighed
"I am Ruth thine handmaid." Boaz lay quite still
And all the red firmament swung round
Over his head; and at this stillness Ruth
Rose, and stretched out herself, and clung to him
Like a long ivy, and he touched her hair.
He raised his eyes at that; and lo, its gold
Shone in the moon, the world's inheritance
Unloosed about her face: incredible hoard!
Boaz whose life was pennies up till then
Fingered her hair, her wealth, her loveliness;
And saw her eyes had two half-moons in them,
And that her breast was very fair and white;
And drawing down her garment to its hem
Boaz whispered to Ruth, "Tarry this night!"

> "Not by day and not by darkness,
> Not by truth," sang Ruth, "nor falsehood,
> Not to play and not in earnest
> I come to you, my love.

81

Through a sort of sleeping twilight,
With a smile as of adventure,
Though I come to lie beside you,
I bless you not, my love.

For the slanted world about us
And the secretness within us
And the distance long between us
Leave little place for love.

You will find me not in darkness
Nor the wise and open daylight,
But a space inside the sunrise
Was given me for love."

"This is no time for singing, Ruth!" complained
The man with difficult and mumbling tongue,
Who had heard her out with only half an ear
And no mind to discern her subtleties.
But Ruth drew back, as distant as her song,
And Boaz found that the meek maid was strong.
Great was the power of that lovely woman:
When it had raised his frenzy, it allayed.
Dream or no dream, wife or no wife, woman
Or spirit, or a being of the earth,
Boaz stood at Ruth's doorway and he sought
Instant admittance. And she quieted him.
The Moabite, the proselyte, this Ruth
Laid a restraining hand on Israel
And to his pleading she spoke mightily.

"Boaz, remember yourself! Think what you are!
To you God gave the legend of a saint;
Men ought to sing of Boaz near and far
And praise his steadfastness and his restraint!

Boaz, remember yourself! Your seed shall be
Kings among kings; for to Prince Boaz's race
The Lord affirmeth throne and majesty:
Spill not that seed in an unhallowed place!

Boaz, remember me! I am no light
Gleaner; I am a woman of some fame,
Born royally in Moab, and tonight
Seeking the promise of far greater name:

I shall not cast my legend down, nor pour
Myself away like wine on a barn floor."

Then truly did the waves break over Boaz
And the bitter waters tumble over him.
And the bitterest of all our feelings, shame,
Drowned out desire as a wave of the sea;
And Boaz wept: to think Ruth mastered him
Not by the spirit of evil, as it was
In the dream he dreamt of her; but by the power
Of good, had Ruth met Boaz in the night
And had prevailed. When Boaz spoke again
It was with a great bitterness of soul,
But not in doubt; but very wearily.

"Forgive me, Ruth," he said to her. And she
Again the meek thing that she was, replied,
"My lord, I am Ruth your servant. Spread your skirt
Over your servant, for indeed you are
Closely akin to me." And Boaz spoke
In a voice made soft for him by weariness,
"May Heaven bless you, for you did choose me
And did not look upon a younger man:
I am your kinsman. Then shall I not do
All that my Ruth requires? Tarry this night:
May you be mine by virtue of this night!
As the Lord lives, after morning comes
I shall redeem you. I am an old man,
I think I have not very long to live.
But by my faith, you may be comforted,
Before tomorrow night you shall be wed:
Boaz is yours, now, Ruth, living or dead."

IV
RUTH

If a man has died, shall you mourn?
If he died before his time,
If he died by fire or by flood,
Or before he was born,
Or by the spilling of blood,
Or if he died because of committing a crime—
Then you shall mourn.

If a man has died, shall you weep?
If he died by earthquake or plague,
Or under a wild beast,
Or if the man had been hideously diseased,
Or died by mistake,
Or passed away unexpectedly in his sleep—
Then you shall weep.

If a man has died shall you wail,
Shall you sit shiva?
If he died from hunger or thirst,
Yes; if his death was cursed—
If they roasted him very slowly over a flame,
Or they raked his flesh with a comb or a rusty nail
Till his soul quivered
And he called with his last strength upon the Name—
Then you shall wail.

If a man has died at the measure of his days,
And the man was senile and spent
And on his wife's breast, thoroughly well content
He came to death

In the simplest way, by letting go his breath,
Silence the dirgesingers, bid them be gone,
And let the bier be brought, and carried on,
The earth be scattered and the garment torn—
But do not mourn.

"Poor Ruth, poor soul, she is not what she was,"
Sighed one wife to another, when the last
Wine had been downed at Boaz's funeral;
"She seems to walk on twigs—and she looks her age—
And her hair does not shine as it did—and her eyes
   go dark—
And she does not dress as well."

                              "They say Naomi
Dresses her."

                    "Could Ruth have admitted this?
Do you think she is sick in body as in mind?
Might she be with child by Boaz?"

                              "I think it likely
Considering—may he rest in peace—the manner
Of Boaz's death."

                         "It will not be Ruth's fault
If she bear no child; she hath paid in advance for
   a son;

Not for the wealthiest bridegroom in the East
Would I have in my mind's eye such a night!"

"With the widow Ruth I spoke but yesterday
And very gently, mindful of her past,
I said, 'Our ancestress Tamar was married,
And her husbands died, and she received for them
Pity and consolation when they died,
And she was comforted, and she bore sons.'"

"What did Ruth say?"

                    "She stared me up and down,
She was the queen, I but a convict slave,
And she cracked out in tones as flat as a whip,
'Is it not enough that I grieve over mine own,'
Said she in that Moab brogue of hers, 'but you
Come to remind me now of the grief of Tamar?'"

"We ought not to encourage that poor pagan
With tales of Tamar, for the marriage-law is fixed;
In our time, twice a widow means for life
If both men died of a so-called natural cause."

"It's God's way, when He comes to chastisement,
(Not without cause, He could not act without cause)
To hit at once on the appropriate thing;
Ruth seemed so peculiarly fit for marrying."

"It was a bitter day for Boaz when
He met the heathenish woman."

                      "Would Boaz agree,
God rest him? He would not. You know how he
    talked
Like a man gone mad of his legend and his son
Which if Ruth bear, she would prove herself in
    his eyes
Though she slay him ten times over . . . in such wise."

"Against my will I credit his legend now;
But its proof is not far off. If Ruth's with child
And she bear Boaz a son, then the rest of the story
Of King—of Messiah—will equally come true,
Whatever we say."

                "Well, not in our day. Peace with you."

"Unto you peace. Indeed, it is very odd."

    "Ruth, will you not be comforted?"
    "Mother, I will not."
    "What would your husband say if he were not
        dead?"
    "Nothing but that I have and he has not
    What he begot."
    "Ruth, are you a fairweather friend of God?"

"What way am I to praise this murderer
My son?"
                        "—That is His chosen one as well."
"Is it not possible I might prefer
My husband's character,
Whatever it was, to all the yarns they tell
Of his redwrinkled and incredible son
God wants to pin a crown and future on?"

"You are the instrument of a great good."
"I am a most mishandled instrument,
Capable of much music, were my wood
Ripened and sheltered and my pegs not bent;
But now I twang, as any woman would,
With what I underwent
When maids and houseboys midwifed unto me
And my husband met the death of a drone bee."

From Boaz until David came, Ruth slept
While the world worked, saw, sorrowed and begot,
And Obed and Jesse were her sons, but not,
Not for the likes of these have women wept.
Then David came, and David was made king;
Anointed, not proclaimed; by Samuel,
Saul's ancient prophet, that had abandoned Saul;
And one brought word to Ruth of it, of how
Samuel swore each man to secrecy
Because of Saul, looped up his tangling cloak,

Uttered a prayer, and disappeared from sight.
"What prayer was that, my son?"
                              "One I had never heard before."
"The words?"
                    "Grant glory, God, unto Thy people;
To those that fear Thee, praise; and a good hope
To those that seek Thee; grant the opening
Of every mouth of those that wait for Thee:
Joy to Thy land, and to Thy city joy;
And to the son of Jesse a full horn,
A full and shining light to David his son
In our time speedily. Amen."
                                            "Amen."

        "Open the mouths that wait for Thee:
        Let mine be one, and not dismayed:
        I see the future, and must be
        Less proud for David than afraid:
        One king of flesh and blood we had:
        What pleasantness has he enjoyed?
        Consider Saul, the self-betrayed!
        A name made great is a name destroyed.

        Who sets himself up privily
        As better than God's handimaid
        The holy Torah: look and see
        His carcass at the crossroads laid!
        Better for that man had he made
        His Torah all, himself a void:

His Torah might have been his trade.
A name made great is a name destroyed.

If so-and-so first say to me,
'Rise up! Be royally arrayed!'
He has no like for villainy
And should be smothered in his bed;
But now I'm king, if that one said,
'Enough, Sir King! Now, step aside!'
—A kettle of hot stuff on his head!
A name made great is a name destroyed.

David! The king must be obeyed
Not by the servants he employed,
But by his own ill spirit, pride!
A name made great is a name destroyed.

"His time has come. And shall Ruth stand amazed?
Or shall Ruth feign honest bewilderment?
But royal blood has found out royal blood
Long since, and knew the king: for ill, for good.
I am not one to dazzle at a crown;
This crown, invisible and difficult
Like Israel itself, distresses me
For David's sake more than my own. The life
Of souls is in this country's atmosphere,
Its throne is not like others. Has my son,
He too, some measure of transparency

So as to prove of one piece with the throne?
Our ruler must primarily remain
On good terms with the ruler of the world
(Meaning, of course, in Israel's case, with God):
Here David undeniably excels.
Boaz found Heaven in the air he breathed,
And David's mouth is ever at God's ear.
David invokes some common formula
To call in God at will, some easy word:
'Lord, into Thine hands I commit my spirit:'
Which each of us says nightly, and by rote,
Seldom with an equivalent success!
David is so familiar with God
Much of the time he never thinks of Him;
We outsiders, we overconsiderate ones,
With genuflection do not get so far.
Like a beloved son, used to receiving
What God gives him from everyone, he knows
Nothing of what the gift may have cost God.
Oh, David's prayer goes up delightfully,
Not as a burden to him, but a song.
Not from compulsion, not from fear, but love,
David fulfils the wishes of his God.
If in a moment of lightness he forget
There are such things as God's commandments writ,
And he break one—or two or three at a time—
What then does David do? David repents.
With such abandon, with such flowering
Of true repentance does the boy repent
The Lord forgives him for his rhetoric.

David cries out to God from the heart's depths:
He is not insincere at any time;
Without duplicity, and without guile,
Quite blanketed in sackcloth, on his knees:
'Acquit me or demean me, O my God,
One way or the other, quickly, at Thy will—
Whichever it is, to Thee, Lord, I shall sing!'
—And gift of singing David had from me.
What all neglect to take into account
Is that from Moab grew, significantly,
His leaping spirit—and his loveliness.
Let him in the daytime give himself to Boaz,
To heroism, government, or war;
But in the nighttime he's for music and song
For those are mine. His charm—I likewise know,
But as a sin most subtly dangerous
To his friends, his nation, and his character.
Has David the wisdom to restrain his power,
The charm I gave him? Ah, mighty it is,
But not enough to rule a country with.
The regent of this state's not only king
But hath, in many a creditable source,
Been named Messiah. Can my son be this?
Where are his traits to serve as witnesses?
What is Messiah? He is more than me.
Glory was never granted to a soul
Because of my so decorative traits.
He must be more than Boaz, who played well,
Consummately well, his part as ancestor.
He must be more than our best virtues fused,

For at their best, David inherits these,
But at their best, these are inadequate.
Whom might we find more royally equipped
Than David? Lived there ever such a one?
Never in this world! Shall a man be born
And have no spot in him? Since charm's a flaw
In its temptations and its consequence,
Yet no man's soul completed, without charm:
Messiah then is a denial of fact.
All rests with God: this too may come to pass;
It must be possible, or prophecy
Had been proved false at the beginning of time,
And prophecy is known for coming true.
When is Messiah? Not till the future to come.
Reason will not abide the thought of him
In a present tense. Boaz could prophesy,
Being, as I have said, the ancestor.
For a dead Boaz, David is Messiah.
Messiah is salvation for our children's
Children's children's children, never for us.

The most I can allow to an old song
Is that Messiah will be seed of David.
He will rise up, perfectly wise and strong,
But not find Ruth here waiting to be saved:
Shall I have more of life than Moses had,
And Moses born a Jew? I am not young;
But sooner than court imperfection
I will, on several counts, arraign my son:

Who knows as I know David's good and bad?
For David is not perfect like the song.

I shall spread out my skirts, and sit, and wait.
This is what I have done, what I will do;
My soul's chief function; in an infirm state
I am not eager to begin anew;
Better wait on, as at my father's house
When I was too unripe to know what for;
As all that summer for Boaz, hours on hours,
Till I might lead him in his own front door;
As more than half a century I waited
First for the birth, then for the proof of David.

Whom do I wait for now? For David's seed?
Even my people might not live so long!
Sense of the ultimate is what I need
And no more to be bankrupt by a song.
Truly, the one for whom I wait is God.
Bethlehem doubts not I have known for years,
Familiarly, my Maker's wide abode,
His columned house, His many-winding stairs.
I met Him once, while I was on the road:
When our paths cross each other now, we nod.

Does this content me? I am not content.
Naomi left the world well-satisfied;
Yes, though a quarter of her life was spent
In banishment, disgraced by her own flesh,
Poisoned, degraded, all-impoverished,

She was fulfilled the day I married Boaz,
Comforted when he died, and by the birth
Of his son marvellously rejustified!
What need she wait for?

                             Lord! And here sit I.
For five and seventy years God's honored guest,
Shielded alike from filth and lowliness,
With fortune as a pagan and a Jew,
Wealthy in one life, wealthier in two.
A pious life was my chief luxury
I built circumference of charity
And I drove evil far away from me;
Whatever poverty I met, I bought;
But I am not contented with the thought.
—What did God mean by ordering my life
Contrary to the suffering in His world?
Beloved are sufferings—so is not Ruth.
Ruth is the stranger, to whom God appears
Formally dighted for some kind of dance!
The spy, to be read censored manuscript!
Or a guest, whom His best parlor will suffice!
Whatever it is, held always at arm's length.
Oh buffet me, Thou never-angry God!
Make me, my God, at one with Israel!
Catch me redhanded, pour, and let me taste
Sharp-edged the wine of retribution!
Your pagan is incapable of sin.
Even the faults that I lament in David,
Find them in me, so I might someway share
His guilt, his comfort, his place at Your ear!

Quietly, Ruth! Though I wait for the Lord
And He continue to hide His face from me,
Has He not waited equally long for Ruth?
Does He wait any the less tolerantly?
Is my part to importune, or command,
Tease Him or fondle Him? Is He a king
Of flesh and blood, that any saucy face
Can force Him to her pleasure? Chivalry
Is not one of my Lord's bright attributes.
He may command me, when He so sees fit.
I am in readiness, and stand alert
Ever since that day on the Bethlehem road
When Naomi, may her soul rest in peace,
Warned me conversion was no easy matter.
I thought she stood upon formality;
I doubt, poor soul, she was herself aware
Of how right she was proved. Instinctively
She warned me. And a Jew is one, I think,
To whose mind some thoughts come instinctively
Without a struggle, almost without name—
Toward which same ends we of the nations aim
Our quiverful of wit and artistry!

I made my choice. There are two sides to the world,
Ever have been, and ever will be two:
That which is Nature's, and that which is God's.
They are kept separate as if by Jordan,
And to go up from Nature's side to God's
Requires no less time than one's very life.
I had what Nature could have offered me,

Beauty, position, equilibrium,
And when I felt there must be something more,
Was it because one cannot trust oneself?
'Then welcome, Nature! Need we more?' I cried,
With my heart never one whit satisfied.

It is not enough. Yes, Nature is, exists.
Nothing upon earth can she create.
Nature's a word we have to designate
The pretty stuff God made us out of mists:
Nature was powerless, He brought to being,
He held, He moved; Nature was acted upon.
He made her various, and Himself One;
Himself for worshiping, Nature for seeing.
Who now will say of Nature, she creates?
Therefore God cannot be at one with her
Innocent symbols. Though He impregnates
A bush or two, makes hills His chancellory,
No part of Nature can a man adore,
No image is, at all, divinity.

For balance, or to give us chance to choose,
A kind of cleft world there will always be.
I took one side, and Orpah kept to the other,
Satisfied with what Nature had to give,
Would not accept four little tears of God!
Nature excited her, variety
Was her bread daily and her wine at night
When she in the most nature-loving way
Slept with the strength of Moab and its flower!

Nature rewarded single-minded Orpah
With everything she had: what Orpah said
When they laid wee Goliath on her knee
And she discerned in him what he became—
I think I know what Orpah said of him!

For Orpah, then, Goliath was Messiah.
What is Messiah but a shoot of Nature?
—Coming full-cry upon the world, demanding
Immediate fulfilment—ah, perfection
At the doorstep waits! Now, Heaven, let him in!
We shall say, Lo, it is here, it is achieved,
Mankind is justified in him; rest,
Rest, my soul, no call for striving now;
He has striven and won, he brings perfection down
For you and you and for all Israel
And for me also! —Doth the Lord wish this?
Only if He would have His world end here!
God has His reasons for making us wait!
A miracle is not created complete
In one fact, in a bolt of thunder-light;
First comes a slow and story-telling time,
Building of thoughts, and birth of character,
And then God's word, given reluctantly!
For every gift worth being granted us
We wait for seasons or for centuries,
And I for David equally as long
As Abraham until his people rose
—Not earlier—in Jacob's dozen sons.

For Ruth, is David the Messiah? No!
All that I am cries No, instinctively!
—But I begin to ask, conceivably
Might living in obedience to perfection
Be one of the last pagan traits in me?
A leaf, a shell, a prettily cut stone
Can be called perfect: what about a man?
Goliath in his way could be called perfect,
Yet David slew Goliath, nor did this
Bring David nearer to perfection.
—Not likely that perfection be confused
With David, when his sins shine visible
To the naked eye for twenty miles about!
Nor will the boy consider himself perfect:
Whatever he is, David is honest in sin.
If he's Messiah, we'll not hear of it
From David's mouth; David will cry out No
Instinctively! But there have been some days
When David rose above perfection
In a way to make perfection irrelevant.
What was it in him when, clad in sheep's skin,
With five smooth stones picked from the running
    brook,
He overmatched Goliath? What, again,
Brought to his harp the sweet expressive note
And the healing word that gave back strength to
    Saul?
Perfection is an outworn metaphor
If only David's figure of speech comes true!
What sent my son out to dismiss the giant?

102

His own brave heart? He might have been brave,
  and died.
David's aim was the Lord's, his cunning the Lord's,
His courage the Lord's; God was then wholly in
  David.
David was God's subjected instrument,
A string He tightened and a harp He bent.

Then David held God, like an earthenware
Vessel of rude make, but it spills no wine.
It is said of vessels, Mind that they be pure,
They must be watched, covered and segregated;
But it is not said, If a certain vessel be chipped
Or not entirely round on its right edge,
It is thereby invalidated! So with men.
We were pure at our devising; if the Lord
Makes use of us, you can depend on Him
To keep us pure enough for Him to use.
As for perfection, that is His concern.
God tests His vessels often enough to learn
David is sturdy, he will spill no wine.
Why under God does David need perfection?
In a most tangible sense, Heaven will be
(Heaven, and not some eloquent shepherd boy)
Ruler in Israel. Enough for me.
—Hath the Lord touched my heart? See, where it
  moves,
Turning itself another way about!
I may indeed believe, by the same token,
God is as close to me as David was

And mocketh me a little, that I knew
Nothing of whom I had been preaching to.

I looked for Him to come from afar off.
I waited for His footstep in the square.
And all the time He was as near to me
As David, and I could not see Him there!

This is what Naomi's text meant by God.
I learn that at the beginning of all, we see
More clearly than again till all is done.
David, David, be not ashamed of me!

I was thick-witted, but ready of heart.
It took the Lord a century to pierce
My stubborn mind, but I would have you write
That though I met with no response for years,

Morning and evening it was my delight
To follow my God's reason out of sight.

Stand forth, Messiah, in my David now:
I sought perfection in the strangest place,
The body of man, and not in my God's grace.
To Thee, Lord, and to Thee alone, I bow.

For David's sake, was God's will brought about?
Or for Ruth's sake, that she with David may

Be crowned by one crown in a single day?
God's mysteries are not past finding out:

Neither for David nor for Ruth, but for
His glory only, hath the Lord done this:
Whatever He does, be sure His reason is
That all men may perceive Him, and adore.

Extolled and blessed be the Name of the Lord:
Honored, exalted, glorified, adored!"